OPRAH WINFREY

SCOTT SANDERS   ROY FURMAN   QUINCY JONES

CREATIVE BATTERY   ANNA FANTACI & CHERYL LACHOWICZ   INDEPENDENT PRESENTERS NETWORK

DAVID LOWY   STEPHANIE P. McCLELLAND   GARY WINNICK   JAN KALLISH

NEDERLANDER PRESENTATIONS, INC.   BOB & HARVEY WEINSTEIN

ANDREW ASNES & ADAM ZOTOVICH   TODD JOHNSON

Present

The Color Purple
A NEW Musical

AND THE WARNER BROS./AMBLIN ENTERTAINMENT MOTION PICTURE

Book by
MARSHA NORMAN

Music and Lyrics by
BRENDA   ALLEE   STEPHEN
RUSSELL   WILLIS   BRAY

Starring

LaCHANZE

ELISABETH WITHERS-MENDES   FELICIA P. FIELDS

BRANDON VICTOR DIXON   RENÉE ELISE GOLDSBERRY   KRISHA MARCANO

and **KINGSLEY LEGGS**

with KIMBERLY ANN HARRIS   MAIA NKENGE WILSON   VIRGINIA ANN WOODRUFF

LOU MYERS   CAROL DENNIS

JEANNETTE I. BAYARDELLE   JAMES BROWN III   ERIC L. CHRISTIAN   LaTRISA A. COLEMAN   BOBBY DÀYE   ANIKA ELLIS

DOUG ESKEW   BAHIYAH SAYYED GAINES   ZIPPORAH G. GATLING   CHARLES GRAY   STEPHANIE GUILAND-BROWN

JAMES HARKNESS   FRANCESCA HARPER   CHANTYLLA JOHNSON   GRASAN KINGSBERRY   CORINNE McFARLANE

KENITA R. MILLER   JC MONTGOMERY   ANGELA ROBINSON   NATHANIEL STAMPLEY   JAMAL STORY   LEON G. THOMAS III

Scenic Design	Costume Design	Lighting Design	Sound Design
JOHN LEE BEATTY	**PAUL TAZEWELL**	**BRIAN MacDEVITT**	**JON WESTON**
Casting	Hair Design	Production Managers	Production Stage Manager
BERNARD TELSEY CASTING	**CHARLES G. LaPOINTE**	**ARTHUR SICCARDI PATRICK SULLIVAN**	**KRISTEN HARRIS**
Press Agent	Marketing		General Management
CAROL FINEMAN/BARLOW·HARTMAN	**TMG - THE MARKETING GROUP**		**NLA/AMY JACOBS**
Music Director	Dance Music Arrangements	Additional Arrangements	Music Coordinator
LINDA TWINE	**DARYL WATERS**	**JOSEPH JOUBERT**	**SEYMOUR RED PRESS**

Orchestrations
JONATHAN TUNICK

Music Supervisor & Incidental Music Arrangements
KEVIN STITES

Choreographed by
DONALD BYRD

Directed by
GARY GRIFFIN

World Premiere Produced by Alliance Theatre, Atlanta, GA
Susan V. Booth, Artistic Director   Thomas Pechar, Managing Director

Cover art courtesy of SpotCo

HAL•LEONARD
CORPORATION

7777 W. BLUEMOUND RD. P.O. BOX 13819 MILWAUKEE, WI 53213

CONTENTS

3   Mysterious Ways

10   Somebody Gonna Love You

12   Our Prayer

18   Big Dog

24   Hell No!

34   Shug Avery Comin' to Town

42   Too Beautiful for Words

45   Push da Button

53   What About Love?

61   Miss Celie's Pants

68   Any Little Thing

74   I'm Here

81   The Color Purple

ISBN-13: 978-1-4234-2612-7
ISBN-10: 1-4234-2612-6

In Australia Contact:
Hal Leonard Australia Pty. Ltd.
4 Lentara Court
Cheltenham, Victoria, 3192 Australia
Email: ausadmin@halleonard.com

Visit Hal Leonard Online at
www.halleonard.com

MYSTERIOUS WAYS

Words and Music by ALLEE WILLIS,
BRENDA RUSSELL and STEPHEN BRAY

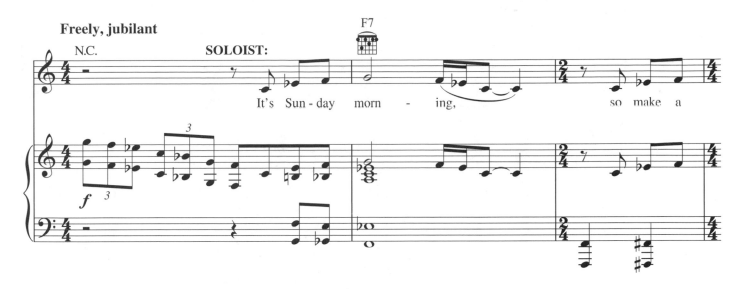

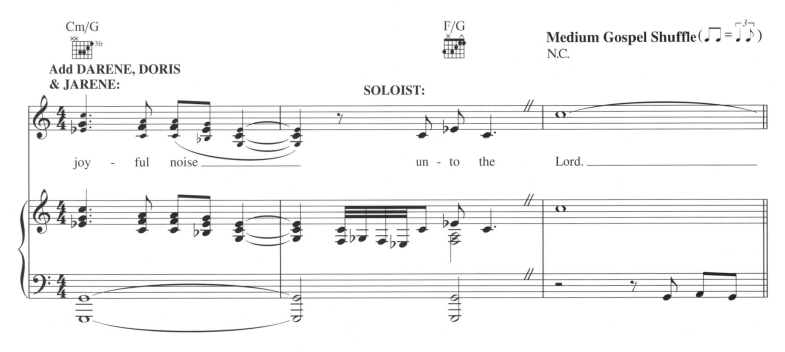

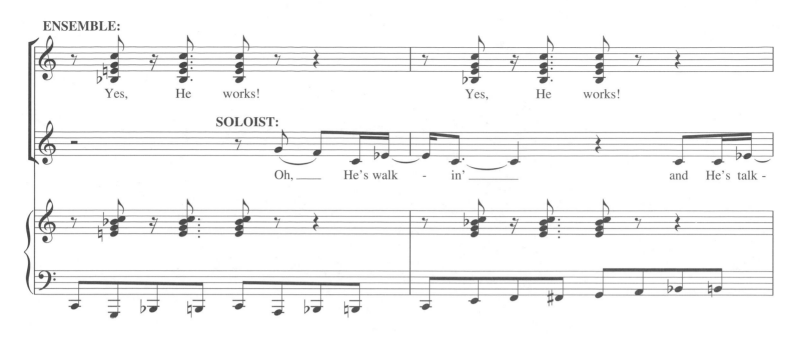

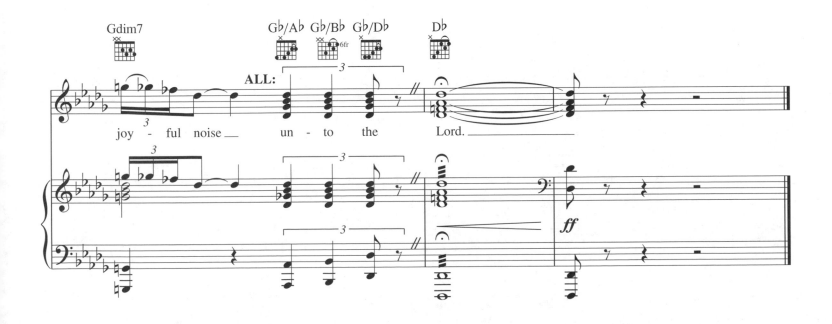

SOMEBODY GONNA LOVE YOU

Words and Music by ALLEE WILLIS,
BRENDA RUSSELL and STEPHEN BRAY

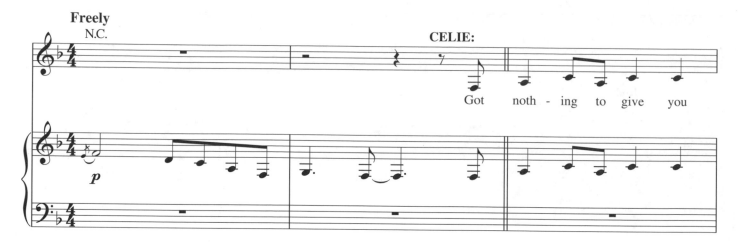

OUR PRAYER

Words and Music by ALLEE WILLIS,
BRENDA RUSSELL and STEPHEN BRAY

BIG DOG

Words and Music by ALLEE WILLIS,
BRENDA RUSSELL and STEPHEN BRAY

all this mess. You know that clean - li - ness ___ next to

humm ___ clean - li - ness ___ next to

god - li - ness! ___

god - li - ness! ___ If you think hard work been dog - gin' you be - fore,

get read - y for the big dog! Hunh! Oww. Net - tie

CELIE:

HELL NO!

Words and Music by ALLEE WILLIS,
BRENDA RUSSELL and STEPHEN BRAY

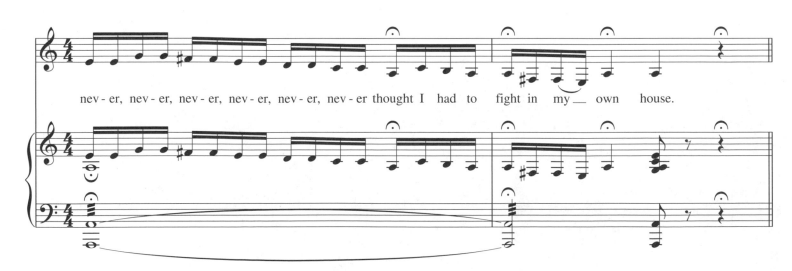

'til you're gone ____

ALL SISTERS:

She be

what he throw - in' a - way,   sis - tah.

gone.   He be wrong.

ALL SISTERS:

Sis - tah,   you   got   to   go. ____

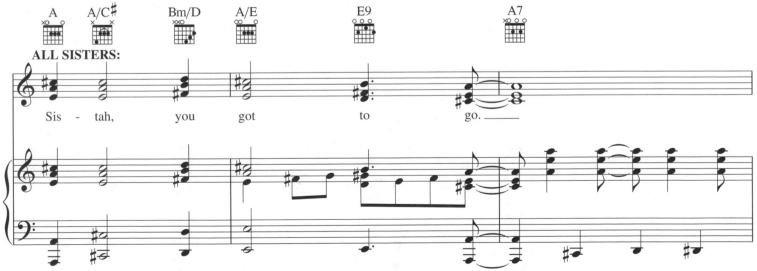

SHUG AVERY COMIN' TO TOWN

Words and Music by ALLEE WILLIS,
BRENDA RUSSELL and STEPHEN BRAY

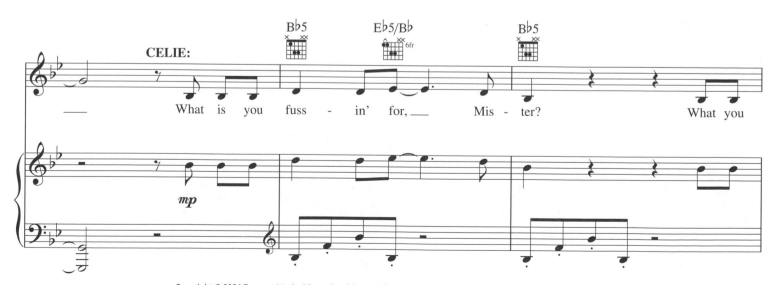

care a-bout __ 'sides your-self? **MISTER:** Ce - lie head _____ full o' rocks. __

There's holes __ in my Sun-day socks. __

(cowbell)

JARENE:
Shug A-v'ry com-in' to town! __

MISTER:
Shug A-v'ry com-in' to town! __

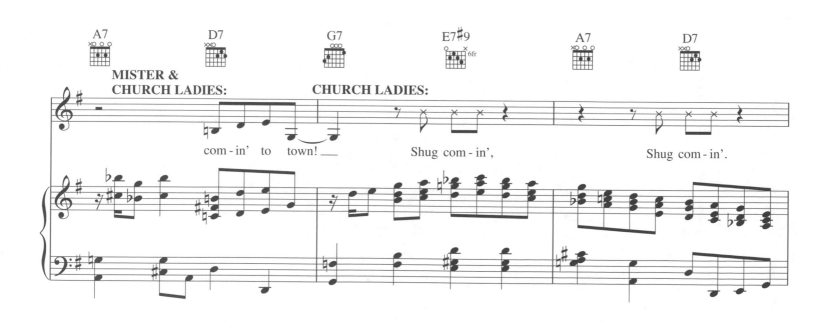

TOO BEAUTIFUL FOR WORDS

Words and Music by ALLEE WILLIS,
BRENDA RUSSELL and STEPHEN BRAY

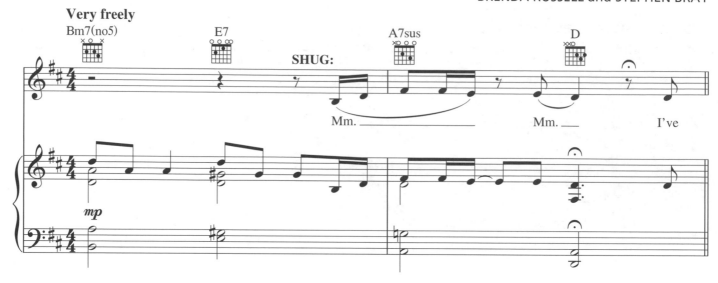

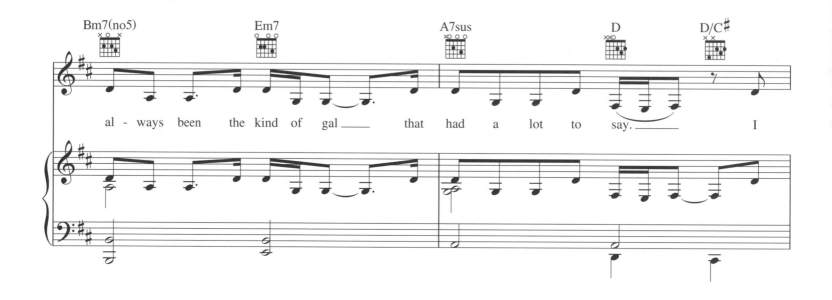

PUSH DA BUTTON

Words and Music by ALLEE WILLIS,
BRENDA RUSSELL and STEPHEN BRAY

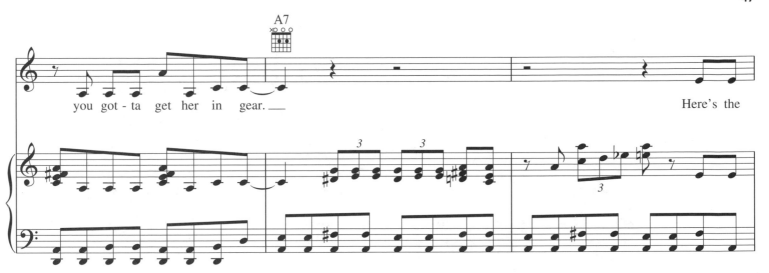

you got-ta get her in gear. ___ Here's the

key to rev her mo-tor, find the spot she love the best. ___ If you don't know where it is, give her the

stick. She'll do the rest. ___ Push da

but - ton.   Push da but - ton.   You got - ta push it if you wan - na come in! __

ENSEMBLE:

Push da but - ton.   Push da but - ton.

Oh, __ push da but - ton.   Give me some - thin'   to let your

Push da but - ton.   Push da but - ton.

ba - by know it ain't __ no sin. __   Now, if you wan - na feel the train a - com - in'

So when to-night you make your lov-er cry out like a li-on roar,__ tell the

neigh-bor your new kit-ty found the cream it look-in' for! __

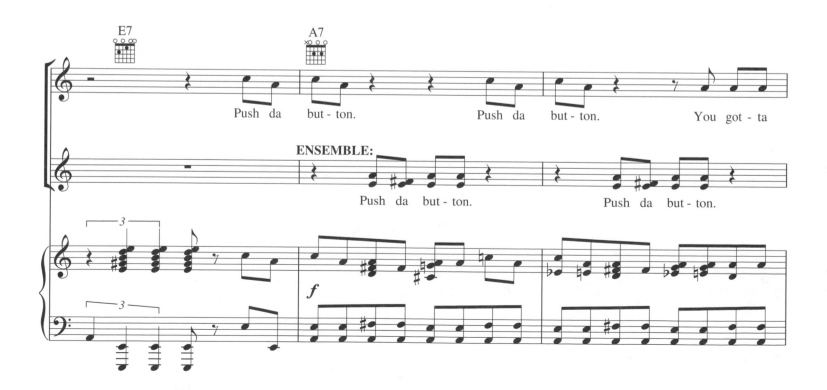

SHUG: Push da but-ton. Push da but-ton. You got-ta

ENSEMBLE: Push da but-ton. Push da but-ton.

push it if you wan - na come in! _____ Push da

but - ton. Give me some - thin' to let your
Push da but - ton. Push da but - ton.

ba - by know it ain't ___ no sin. ___ Now if you

WHAT ABOUT LOVE?

Words and Music by ALLEE WILLIS,
BRENDA RUSSELL and STEPHEN BRAY

MISS CELIE'S PANTS

Words and Music by ALLEE WILLIS,
BRENDA RUSSELL and STEPHEN BRAY

ANY LITTLE THING

Words and Music by ALLEE WILLIS,
BRENDA RUSSELL and STEPHEN BRAY

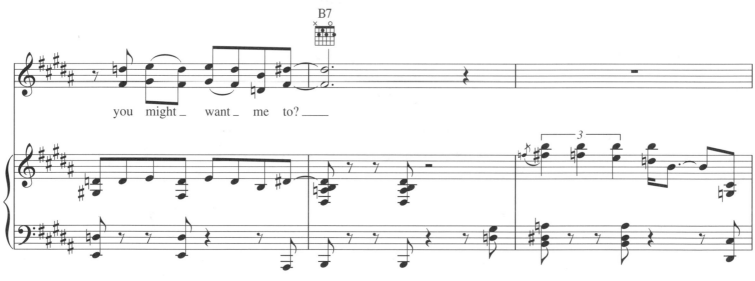

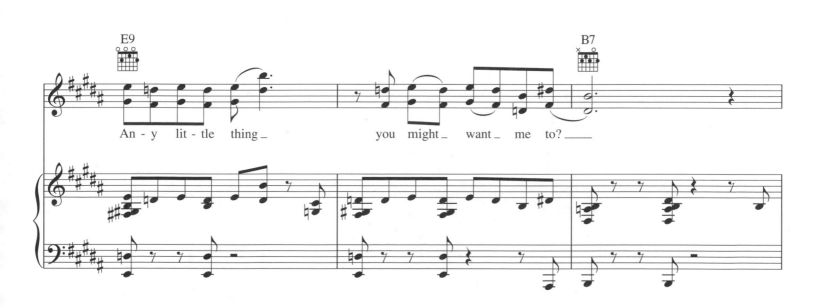

I'M HERE

Words and Music by ALLEE WILLIS,
BRENDA RUSSELL and STEPHEN BRAY

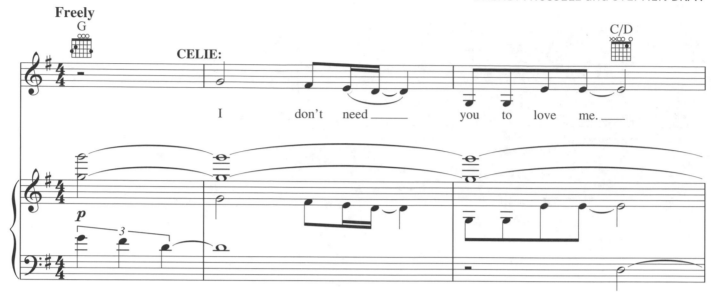

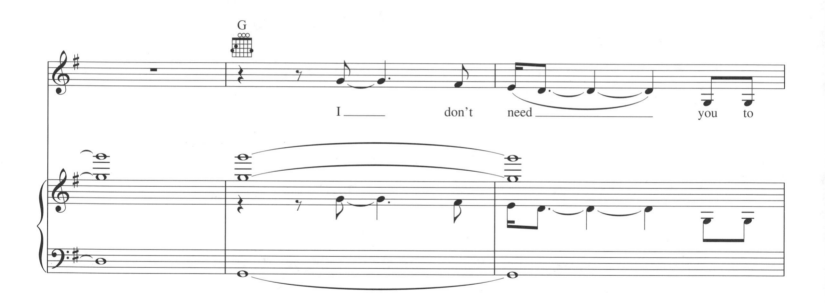

THE COLOR PURPLE

Words and Music by ALLEE WILLIS,
BRENDA RUSSELL and STEPHEN BRAY

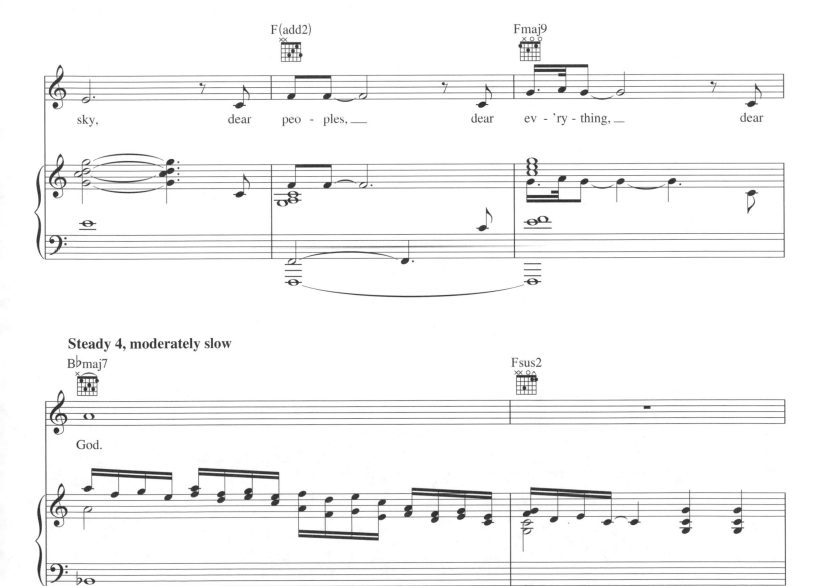